GRAMMAR RAY
PUNCTUATION
& SENTENCES

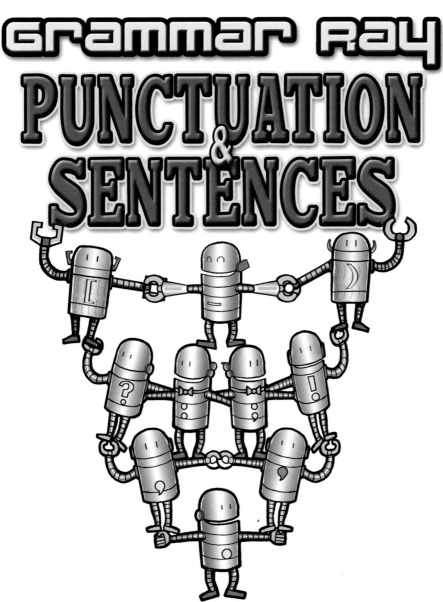

K1

a graphic guide to grammar
andrew carter

Published by Evans Brothers Limited
2A Portman Mansions
Chiltern Street
London W1U 6NR

© in this edition Evans Brothers Limited 2010
© in the text and illustrations Andrew Carter 2010

Printed in Malta by Gutenberg Press

Editor: Bryony Jones
Designer: Mark Holt

British Library Cataloguing in Publication Data

Carter, Andrew.
Punctuation and sentences. — (Grammar Ray)
1. English language—Punctuation—Juvenile literature.
2. English language—Sentences—Juvenile literature.
I. Title II. Series
421.1-dc22

ISBN-13: 9780237538521

contents

INTRODUCTION

Hello and welcome to Grammar Ray! You are
about to enter a world of fun and adventure, where
English grammar is brought to life. Words in the English
language can be divided into different groups called
'parts of speech'. In this title, we will join the robots
in their quest to explore how the parts of speech
fit together to make sentences.

We are the punctuation robots.
Follow us to learn how we make the world
of written English make sense!

The first part of the book is a comic strip.
Join the robots as they demonstrate how the
different punctuation marks work and use
some super-strong conjunctions glue to
join the parts of a sentence together.

After you've followed the robots in
their adventures, the rest of the book looks
at constructing sentences in more detail, and
gives some more examples. Use this if you need
a reminder of the role punctuation and sentences
play in English grammar. It also requires your
puzzle-solving skills and tests what you
have learnt along the way. So be sure
to pay attention!

Before we look at punctuation and sentences, let's start right at the beginning and look at the basics of written English.

In English there are 26 letters in the alphabet.

We combine letters to make words.

words

Every word in English is a *part of speech*. Let's take a look at the most common parts of speech.

Nouns name things e.g. *cat, family, Tokyo, love*

Pronouns can replace nouns e.g. *he, she, they, this*

Adjectives describe nouns e.g. *big, happy, green, many*

Verbs describe physical or mental actions e.g. *jump, play, think, be*

Adverbs describe how something is done e.g. *quickly, well, sadly*

Prepositions tell us about position and movement e.g. *on, at, up*

We combine these parts of speech to make *sentences*.

Conjunctions are the words that join words, phrases and parts of sentences.

asentencedoes notmakesense unlessweusethe followingspaces andpunctuation marks

A sentence does not make sense unless we use the following: spaces and punctuation marks.

So what are punctuation marks?

Punctuation marks are the small symbols that we use to give meaning to sentences and help them to make sense.

Here is a handful of the most common.

Now let's take a look at them individually and see how they can be used...

The full stop

Full stops are great at stopping a sentence.

Full stops are most commonly used to end a sentence:

The robot was hungry.

We also use full stops in abbreviations:

P.S.   J.K. Rowling   P.M.

If the abbreviation contains the first and last letters of the word, you do not need to use full stops:

Mr   Dr   Utd

The exclamation mark

Exclamation marks show emotions easily!

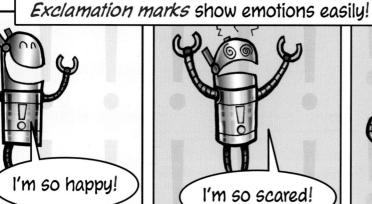

I'm so happy!

I'm so scared!

I'm so angry!

An exclamation mark can be used to end a sentence in a strong, emphasised way:

Help!   Don't eat all the pizza!   This is great!

3. The question mark

Question marks are always asking questions.

Why does the sun shine?

How do you fly?

Why do I ask so many questions?

We use a question mark at the end of a sentence to make it clear that we are asking a question. If we use a question mark we d not need to use a full stop:

How long is a piece of string?

Why did the chicken cross the road?

4. Brackets (also known as parentheses)

Round brackets are great at carrying extra information *[and so are their cousins, square brackets]*.

extra information

Round brackets can contain words that could be taken out of a sentence without changing its meaning, but that carry extra informatic

The rabbit *(who was getting hungry now)* jumped through the gras:

Square brackets are used to add words that clarify or explain the meaning of a sentence without giving extra information:

She looked up at the hero *[Verb-Man]* as he flew across the sky.

. The comma

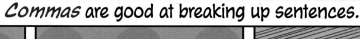

Commas are good at breaking up sentences.

CRINK!

CRACK!

We use a comma to break up a sentence and give a short pause
within it, e.g.

Although it was tiny, the caterpillar ate a huge leaf by itself.

The dog, which was barking noisily, chased after its own tail.

A comma is also used to separate adjectives in a sentence, e.g.

A giant, black, evil monster towered over the scared villagers.

Another use for commas is to separate items in a list, e.g.

*The magician reached into his hat and pulled out a white rabbit,
a small monkey, a can of fizzy drink and a packet of seeds.*

Also use a comma when you address somebody by their name, e.g.

Hello, Verb-Man!

Show us a trick, Magnificent Pronoun!

6. The apostrophe

Apostrophes are very good at two particular tasks.

1. They can be used to show that one or more letters are missing, e.

it's = it is   don't = do not   I'll = I will

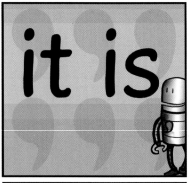

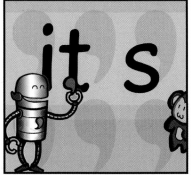

2. Used with an 's', they can tell us that something belongs to someone, e.g.

the dog's bone

Verb-Man's ice cream

the magician wand

Colons are very good at introducing lists.

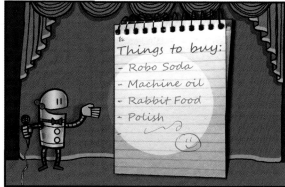

We can use colons to introduce a list or bullet points, e.g.

He describes himself with three words: cool, handsome and modest.

Punctuation marks that we use to end a sentence:

- *Full stop*
- *Question mark*
- *Exclamation mark*

We also use them to join two statements when the second statement explains the first one, e.g.

The Incredible Noun performed tricks: he explained what nouns were.

The man transformed into his alter ego: he became Verb-Man.

Colons are also used to introduce a quotation, e.g.

The clown whispered to the ringmaster: "Does my hair look funny?"

8. Quotation marks

> *Quotation marks* are very useful to repeat other people's words.

When we want to show that something has been said by someone, we can use *quotation marks*. There are double (" ") and single (' ') marks but there is no big difference in their meaning.

"I'm rather hungry," the greedy cat grumbled aloud to himself.
'It's time to leave,' whispered the two startled mice.

When you write direct speech, remember the following things: Always start a new line when a new person starts speaking, e.g.

'Who's that?' asked the boy.
'That's Verb-Man!' answered his friend.

Before you close or re-open quotation marks, include punctuation, e.

'Yes,' he said, 'I am Verb-Man.'
'Woof!' barked the dog.
She asked, 'Where?'

You should also use *quotation marks* to show that text has come from another written source such as a book or magazine and also for song titles.

Gazing up at the night sky he hummed
'Twinkle, Twinkle, Little Star'.

Hyphens are great at connecting things.

Hyphens have several uses:

1. They can join certain words and numbers together, e.g.

T-shirt   forty-two   vice-president

2. They can link words to create compound adjectives, e.g.

A red, bearded robot = a red robot with a beard.

By adding a hyphen you can change the meaning.

A red-bearded robot = a robot with a red beard.

3. They can connect one part of a word to the other if it is split across two lines, e.g.

*Verb-Man flew into the sky, his jets streak-
ing behind him. Far below the rescued villagers waved and cheered.*

10. The semi-colon

Semi-colons create longer pauses than commas.

Use a semi-colon to link two sentences without using a word like 'and' or 'but':

He opened the box; there was a strange glow inside.
The robot was thirsty; he bought a drink.

Semi-colons can also be used like commas to separate things in a li...

In the box he found: a hat; a wand; a bow tie and a rabbit.

11. The ellipsis

Ellipses like to build suspense.

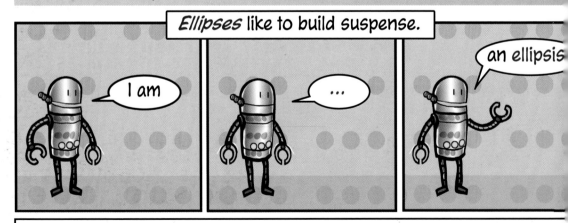

I am

...

an ellipsis

An *ellipsis* can be used to end a sentence to suggest that words have deliberately been missed out, so it is often used to build suspense, e...

She would only have one bullet to stop the monster:
she aimed her pistol, pulled the trigger and...

CONJUNCTIONS GLUE

- **Extra Strength** ✓
- **Long Lasting** ✓
- **Rapidly bonds parts of speech** ✓

UNIQUE NEW FORMULA

Sticks nouns, verbs, adverbs pronouns, prepositions and adjectives!

Net Weight 10g

Net Weight 10g

Net Weight 10g

Conjunctions are the words that we use to join words, phrases and parts of sentences.

Did you know that conjunctions are often also called connectives?

although

and

as

but

Here are some of the most common conjunctions:

since

because

Let's take a look at how conjunctions are used in some sentences.

CONJUNCTIONS *GLUE*

Instructions for use:

Ensure that any parts of speech are clean and free of any dirt, dust or grease, but make sure they are not wet. Apply Conjunctions Glue to a word, phrase or part of a sentence and connect it to another. Hold firmly together for a few seconds to form an initial bond, leave for a further 10 minutes to enable the glue to dry completely.

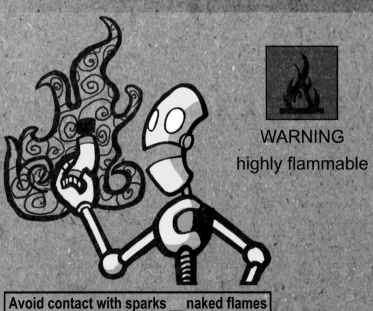

WARNING
highly flammable

WARNING
do not touch

Made in England
33ml

1 0271X0 157803

Avoid contact with sparks __ naked flames

sentences

**A sentence is made up of different parts of speech.
You use them like building blocks to make a complete sentence.**

Let's start the sentence with a noun (**fox**) and an article (**the**).

The fox is the main focus of the sentence so it become known as the '*subject*'. The subject usually comes first in a sentence.

FOR EXAMPLE:

The fox

Now add a verb (**jumps**) after the subject to explain wh the fox is doing.

Now that we have a subject and a verb we have a complete sentence.

FOR EXAMPLE:

The fox jumps.

Many sentences contain more than just a subject and a verb. They usually contain an '*object*' too. An object is a noun that is having the verb of the sentence done to it. So in this sentence the **dog** is the object. It is being jumped over.

Of course, we need to add an article (the) to the noun (**dog**) so that the sentence makes sense.

Finally we can add a preposition (over) to explain the fox's movement further.

This sentence now contains a subject (The fox), a verb (jumps), a preposition (over) and an object (the dog).

R EXAMPLE:

The *fox jumps over* **the** *dog.*

Many sentences contain more than just a subject, verb and object. Finally we can add more information about the **fox** and the **dog** by adding some adjectives (**brown, lazy** and **grey**). We can add an adverb (**quickly**) to describe how the **fox jumped**.

R EXAMPLE:

The brown *fox jumps* **quickly** over **the** lazy, grey *dog.*

The final sentence is called a *pangram* because it contains all the letters of the alphabet. Can you spot them all?

punctuation & sentences
test yourself

1. What is the name of each punctuation mark?

(a) ?   (b) ;   (c) " "   (d) '   (e) -

2. Which conjunction best completes the sentence?

The robot was glad that his new arms had arrived,
_____ he felt there might have been some mistake.

(a) because

(b) since

(c) however

(d) or

REPLAC
ARM

3. Arrange the words into a sentence.

vegetarian The drank juice vampire the thirstily tomato.

Turn the page upside-down to see the answers!

INDEX

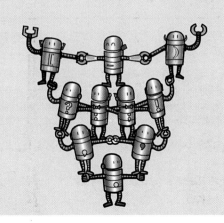

enjoy more of the wonderful world of

Grammar Ray

Grammar Ray
ADJECTIVES

a graphic guide to grammar
andrew carter

ISBN: 9780237538491

Grammar Ray
ADVERBS

a graphic guide to grammar
andrew carter

ISBN: 9780237538507

Grammar Ra
NOUNS & PRONOUNS

a graphic guide to gramm
andrew carter

ISBN: 97802375376

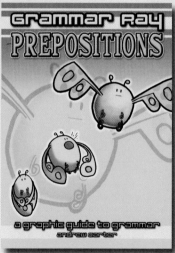

Grammar Ray
PREPOSITIONS

a graphic guide to grammar
andrew carter

ISBN: 9780237538514

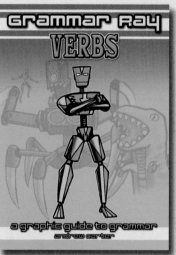

Grammar Ray
VERBS

a graphic guide to grammar
andrew carter

ISBN: 9780237538484